SCHOOL JOKES

Compiled and Illustrated by
Viki Woodworth

Text copyright © 1991 by The Child's World, Inc.
All rights reserved. No part of this book may be
reproduced or utilized in any form or by any means
without written permission from the Publisher.
Printed in the United States of America.

Distributed to Schools and Libraries
in the United States by
ENCYCLOPAEDIA BRITANNICA EDUCATIONAL CORP.
310 S. Michigan Avenue
Chicago, Illinois 60604

Library of Congress Cataloging-in-Publication Data
Rothaus, James.
School jokes / Jim Rothaus; compiled and illustrated by Viki Woodworth.
p. cm.
Summary: A collection of jokes relating to school.
Example: Why does the elephant do so well in school?
She has lots of gray matter.
ISBN 0-89565-726-0
1. Schools—Juvenile humor. 2. Wit and humor, Juvenile.
[1. Schools—Wit and humor. 2. Jokes.] I. Title.
PN6231.S3R678 1991   91-17333
818'.5402—dc20   CIP / AC

SCHOOL JOKES

Compiled and Illustrated by
Viki Woodworth

THE CHILD'S WORLD

Father: Why did you flunk history, son?
Son: I let bygones be bygones.

What is the difference between a school bus driver and a cold?
One knows the stops, and the other stops the nose.

What do you get when you cross an absent-minded teacher with an insect?
A forget-me-gnat.

Why does the elephant do so well in school?
She has lots of gray matter.

What do you get when you cross a book of nursery rhymes with an orange.
Mother Juice.

What's the best way to pass a geometry test?
Learn all the angles.

Why does the school cafeteria serve alphabet soup?
So students can eat and read at the same time.

Mother: I'm worried dear, about you being at the bottom of your class.
Son: Don't worry, Mom. They teach the same stuff at both ends.

Mother: What did you learn in school today?
Daughter: How to talk without moving my lips.

Joe: Do you write with your left hand or right hand?
Moe: My right hand.
Joe: You do? Strange, I use a pen.

Where do you find smart hot dogs?
On the honor roll.

How did the Vikings send messages?
In Norse Code.

Why was the straight "A" student always running?
She was pursuing her studies.

What is a lion's favorite period of history?
The Roaring Twenties.

Why did the balloon do so well in school?
It went right to the top of the class.

What is NBC?
The wrong way to start the alphabet.

What school has a sign that says, "Please don't knock"?
Karate school.

How many months have 28 days?
All of them.

Suzie: I won a prize in school today. The teacher asked how many legs a hippo had. I said three.
Dad: Three? How did you win?
Suzie: I came the closest.

What happened to the bad egg at school?
It got egg-spelled.

Why did the little witch flunk out of school?
She couldn't spell.

Teacher: What is the best way to prevent infection caused by biting insects?
Pupil: Don't bite any.

What's the emptiest row in school?
The zero.

How was the calf's report card?
Grade A.

What is yellow, has lots of wheels and lies on its back?
A dead school bus.

If General Custer were alive today, what would he be famous for?
His age.

Son: I'm glad you call me Jason, Dad.
Dad: Why?
Son: Because that's what the kids at school call me.

Where did knights study dragon fighting?
In knight school.

Whose figure can't you see?
A figure of speech.

What's one and one?
Two.
What's six minus four?
Two.
Who wrote *Tom Sawyer*?
Twain.
Now say all the answers together.
Two, Two, Twain.
Have a nice twip.

What kind of bug does well in English?
A spelling bee.

What geometric angle is never wrong?
A right angle.

Where is Timbuktu?
Right between Timbuk-one and Timbuk-three.

Jessica: Dad will you do my homework for me?
Dad: No, it wouldn't be right.
Jessica: It's not right when I do it either.

Who was the smartest pig in the world?
Ein-swine.

What book has lists of famous owls?
Who's Who.

How many feet are there in the world?
Twice the number of people.

What is red, white and blue and says, "Ouch"?
Betsy Ross, sewing the flag, without her eyeglasses.

Why do bankers go to art school?
To draw interest.

Student: I was so close to the right answers on the math test.
Other Student: Really?
Student: Yes, they were only two desks away.

Where do they keep prehistoric cows?
In a moo-seum.

How do we know Napoleon loved spicy food?

He mustard (mustered) his army and salted (assaulted) the city.

Father: How were the exam questions?
Son: The questions were easy, but the answers were really hard!

A class has a top and a bottom. What lies between?

The student body.

Why shouldn't you add too many numbers on a hot day?

You might get sumstroke.

What did George Washington become when he was 38 years old?

39.

What do cheerleaders learn at school?

The three Rs. Rah! Rah! Rah!

What kind of poetry do you make up out of your head?

Blank verse.

Why did the two-headed monster do so well in school?
Two heads are better than one.

Dad: Why are you failing in history?
Daughter: They only ask about things that happened before I was born.

What happens when you throw a black rock into the Red Sea?
It gets wet.

What is a snake's best subject?
History.

What can you find in the Great Wall of China that wasn't there originally.
Cracks.

Student: What is an archaeologist?
Other Student: Someone whose job is in ruins.

Why did the teacher excuse the little firefly?
When you gotta glow, you gotta glow.

What type of school shoes does a bee wear?
Buzzter Browns.

Dad: What did you learn today?
Daughter: How to write.
Dad: Great! What did you write?
Daughter: I'm not sure. I haven't learned how to read.

If you took the school bus home, what would happen?
Your dad would make you return it!

What part of a book is like a fish?
The fin-ish.

What school teaches you how to drive tanks?
Tank U.

Why did the owl flunk out of school?
It didn't give a hoot.

Mother: What did you learn in school today?
Son: Not enough. I have to go back tomorrow.

What kind of schoolwork do elves have?
Gnomework.

Student: Our school just played Straus.
Jock: Who won?

If you wanted to make a bucket of water weigh less, what could you add?
Holes.

Why was the firefly such a good student?
It was very bright.

First I had tonsillitis, followed by appendicitis and pneumonia, ending with neuritis. Then they gave me hypodermic and innoculation.
Boy did you have a hard time.
I'll say, I never thought I'd pass that spelling test.

What is raised in Spain during the rainy season?
Umbrellas.

Student: What has 87 legs, a lavender body and pink polka dots?
Other Student: I don't know. What does?
Student: I don't know either, but there's one crawling on you.

Why does a duck get straight "A's" in school?

It's a wise quacker.

What takes bees to school?
A school buzz.

1st Student: What time do you wake up?
2nd Student: About an hour and ½ after I get to school.

What is the beginning of a duck book?
The intro-duck-tion.

What do you get if you cross one principal with another principal?
Don't do it! Principals don't like to be crossed.

Why do snobs like books?
Because they have titles.

What do you call the back door of the cafeteria?
The bacteria.

What does a monkey learn in school?
The Ape B Cs.

**What kind of tests do witches have
in school?**
Hex-aminations.

Why did the germ cross the microscope?
To get to the other slide.

Why does the school clock scratch itself?
It has ticks.

Why did the mosquito stay up all night?
Studying for his blood test.

What school makes all its students drop out?
Parachute school.

Why is the pen mightier than the sword?
Because no one invented a ballpoint sword.

Why did Freddie put a frog on the teacher's desk?
Because he couldn't find a spider.

Father: Aren't you first in anything at school?
Son: Sure, dad, I'm always first in the lunch line.

Why are clocks always tired?
Because they're always running.

If two's company and three's a crowd, what's four and five?
Nine.

How did the pilgrims sleep on the Mayflower?
With their eyes closed.

Why did the bird get thrown out of class?
For peeping during a test.

What do vampires learn in business school?
How to type blood.

Why is a giant such an awful student?
His head is always in the clouds.

Do snakes know their multiplication tables?
No, they're all adders.

Principal: What are you going to be when you get out of school?
Pupil: An old man.

How can you tell when a fish plays hookey?
It isn't in a school.

After her first day of school, Maryanne came home and announced:
"It was boring, some lady couldn't spell 'dog,' so I told her how."

What bet can never be won?
The alphabet.

What is the worst thing in the school cafeteria?
The food.

Who's the meanest singer in history?
Attila the Hum.

Why was the clock in the library?
It tocked too much.

Why is a pickle good in school?
It uses its brine.

How many seconds are there in a year?
Twelve. January 2nd, February 2nd, March 2nd,
April 2nd, May 2nd, June 2nd, July 2nd, August 2nd,
September 2nd, October 2nd, November 2nd,
December 2nd.

Mom: How did you find school today?
Son: Oh, I just got off the bus—and there it was!

**After Laurie's first day of school she told
her mother,**
"It was OK, except for some old lady named Teacher.
She kept ruining all our fun."

Why did everyone race out of the library?
Someone found "dynamite" in the dictionary.

What angle is the prettiest?
Acute angle.